Decoy 24

A Glimpse at the Undercover Operations of Law Enforcement

James R. Davis

Criminologist

www.Decoy24.com

Creative Team Publishing
Ft. Worth, Texas

Disclaimer:

The opinions and conclusions expressed are solely of the author and/or the individuals represented, and are limited to the facts, experiences, and circumstances involved. Many of the stories herein are accurate or based on actual events. Certain names, locations, and related circumstances have been changed to protect confidentiality and insure anonymity of officers, victim-witnesses, and suspects. Due diligence has been exercised to obtain written permission for use of references or quotes where required. Additional quotes or references are subject to Fair Use Doctrine. Where additional references or quotes require source credit, upon written certification that such claim is accurate, credit for use will be noted on this website: www.Decoy24.com. Any resemblance to past or current people, places, circumstances, or events is purely coincidental.

ISBN: 978-0-9979519-0-5

PUBLISHED BY CREATIVE TEAM PUBLISHING
www.CreativeTeamPublishing.com
Ft. Worth, Texas

Printed in the United States of America

Endorsements

Mr. Davis gives us a heartfelt look into a branch of law enforcement that is often, perhaps justifiably, unknown and unreported. Teaming up with Decoy 24 is an education about what it's like to go undercover. To go there you must be strong of heart, have tough skin, and a keen mind.
~ **Dr. Thomas Keller, Clinical Psychologist**

I have known James for almost ten years. As a police officer, I appreciate the informative and heartfelt conversation both from his book, and in person. Chapter 9 sent chills down my spine knowing how dangerous the situation was … The book is a great read!
~ **Scott Wulfing, Police Officer, City of La Mesa, California**

I worked cases with James R. Davis, a.k.a. Decoy 24. He is professional and a "nose to the grindstone" kind of guy. His stories will amaze you, and enlighten you, too!
~ **Anonymous**

I've been a personal friend and associate of Mr. Davis for over thirty years, attended his seminars, and taught with him at many departments throughout the United States. He is one of a select few trainers that can be called an expert!
~ **Frank Cornetta, Det. Sgt. Arson/Bomb Squad, Ret.**
Broward Co. Sheriff's Department, Ft. Lauderdale, Florida

Jim and I have a long and enduring relationship. Cops understand each other. He knows of what he speaks. Buy his book and buy my pocket holsters.
~ **Robert Mika, Police Officer, L.A.P.D,**
Los Angeles, California, Ret.
Chief of Police, Ret., Reads Town, Wisconsin
President, Mika's Pocket Holsters
https://mikaspocketholsters.com/

Asking the Tough Questions

Like going through divorce, death, or the loss of a friendship, when you go undercover you soon feel the dismantling of yourself. You lose close relationships. All that you are ends up being invaded, intruded upon, and without your knowledge or permission. Without a strong intellect, without living a faith-based life lived in service to others, you may very well be doomed to failure.

No matter how hard one tries to protect themselves, once undercover for any long period in time, the portrayed new self, steps in front of the old, original self. The new experiences and fantasies become a new reality. "Lose your edge, lose your cover, you may lose your life." Be very, very careful.

Undercover officers must be trained, and trained well! Practice makes perfect, so some think. Not on your life … perfect practice makes perfect. Whether it is street dialect, dressing for the occasion, i.e., you wear pretty much what the bad guy wears. If the uniform of the day is long hair, then it's long hair. Maybe a beard. Maybe showering less often. Maybe it's using profanity. Cussing is normal and almost recognized as a positive character trait for many

5

hoodlums. You must insulate yourself from suspicion. People will be suspicious and curious no matter what you do.

There was a time when I cut off all social contact with friends for months. I was unable to go to church. Authentic bad guys don't go to church. This was an incredible sacrifice for me. My faith actually made me acutely aware, focused, grounded, and, when "darkness came calling," I breathed deeply and thought to myself, "Bring it on!" I recall a few times sneaking over to a monastery four miles or so from my house. I would sit in the front courtyard, surrounded by flowers and fruit trees, and listen to vespers (evening prayers).

It's been a long journey in this life. I tell officers assigned to undercover operations, or special details with a high probability of risk, to work through challenge and work through the many, many family issues that must be confronted. My children didn't know what I did—even being in law enforcement—until they were in high school. Do things right! Insulate yourself and insulate your family.

I recall an undercover officer who was "surfaced," or found out, when he rushed to the hospital to meet his wife, who was in labor. He was tailed and the bad guys asked if they could get a message to him. One of the medical staff commented that the officer's wife was in labor. That's all it took. This officer ended up compromised and he was an extraordinary UC (undercover) officer.

It's not about being paranoid. It's about being vigilant, keenly vigilant. Divulge what you do to no one. Got it? There is nothing more cavalier than shooting off your mouth. Those who hear you may snitch you off — even innocently if you will — so don't give anyone any information. You might be compromised by a source you never expected. My cover was being an advocate for war veterans, being a graduate student, or hanging out at the beach. (For the reader: I am a Vietnam vet, I did go to graduate and post graduate school, and I still hang out at the beach.) Know what your cover is! Study your role. You may be tested in certain criminal circles. Be able to back up your story. You're an actor, so read the screen play. Don't be unprepared.

James R. Davis

Decoy 24

A Glimpse at the Undercover Operations of Law Enforcement

James R. Davis
Criminologist

Dedication

Dedicated to all the officers on the rolls of LEOKA* and their families. Also to all those who are assigned to special investigations details and may not ever be known or heard of.

~ Decoy 24

*(Law Enforcement Officers Killed and Assaulted)

Table of Contents

Table of Contents

*****

*****

Chapter 1
Glassing ... Big Homes

Police agencies across the nation are plagued with crimes committed by gang members—syndicated drug dealers, sex traffic brokers, designer drug manufacturers, street thugs, hood rats, and the list goes on and on. The macro view I gained from doing operations was like looking into a dollhouse. Everything could be seen.

The gang problem has been prevalent since at least the late 1960s. In fifty years, the problem has grown exponentially. Mayors, governors, and presidents all pay appropriate lip service to the issue, but only as a political expedient. At this writing, the mayor of Chicago continues to mumble about how to impact the crisis of homicides in his city. It is a manageable problem; but without political will, true political leadership, nothing can possibly happen.

I will offer two immediate intervention strategies, but neither will be popular to the public unless understood by the public. The first is simply, "Military Support to Civilian Authority." A governor's declaration and in comes the National Guard.

On every street corner, in every part of a community where the insidious crime of murder occurs, where continued drive-by shootings occur, where corner-of-the-block drug sales occur in broad daylight, you need decisive intervention. Programs that work! If you can't sell this program to the public, you shouldn't be in office.

The other is aggressive community-oriented policing. Not to simply put more police in an area driving around in patrol cars, but police stationed on the corners where drug sales and gang members are prevalent.

They need to be polite, professional, caring officers who talk with the public they serve. No gang bangers are going to shuffle down the street and risk conversation with the "po-po", the rollers, the punk police. Initiate vehicle safety checks and DUI checkpoints. Uninsured motorists, those driving with suspended or revoked licenses, stolen vehicles … There will be hundreds of arrests, or at least citations issued and autos impounded. Working with school police to honestly address truancy is critical for school-age youth.

If you are a citizen in a dangerous town and there is no end to the violence, my advice is simple: move! I have advocated this to many citizens in many crime-ridden areas for many years. But I digress…

As the day begins at any police department, or sheriff's department that has a dedicated patrol division (some sheriff's departments provide court services and corrections services only), there will be a morning patrol briefing. Uniformed personnel sit at desks, tables, or in chairs with notebooks, and are informed of recent criminal activity from the previous evening and for the previous five days. It's not just donuts!

These briefings are normally conducted by uniformed patrol supervisors usually holding the rank of sergeant. There are times when someone will be designated as an acting supervisor if a sergeant is not available.

There are also many times when a lieutenant may attend or conduct the briefings. Those personnel are executive command personnel and outrank sergeants. They are commonly known as the Shift Commanders or Watch Commanders for the shift. These individuals manage patrol operations during their tour of duty. They are in contact with the patrol sergeants and patrol officers when necessary.

Briefings entail reviewing arrest reports from previous shifts. BOLOs are discussed (a common phrase for "Be On the Lookout" for certain individuals) as well as stolen vehicle occurrences, home burglaries, and being attentive to homeless persons and their activity. Some homeless people search for shelter while others prowl in shopping centers, snatch purses from unsuspecting shoppers, and, as vagrants do, panhandle.

Dangerous situations such as slippery roadways, snow and ice may be discussed. Reminders of responsibilities around schools—both in the morning and when school is out—like traffic control, safe use of crosswalks, and reminding drivers school zone speed limits are routine, but, nonetheless, important.

Some briefings may include a 10 or 15 minute mini-training session. The topics could range from "How to Speak with Emotionally Disturbed Persons (EDPS)," violent suspect control, departmental policy, smoking privileges by personnel, or possibly discussing departmental policy on emergency police pursuits.

During these briefings there may or may not be information disseminated on a new concealed weapon or a scam to get people to donate for some fraudulent operation. As the lieutenant or the senior officer—literally running the daily patrol operation of a department—returns to their office, the front desk, or the 911 Communications Center, the patrol supervisors and patrol officers head onto the street, relieving the night watch.

Fresh personnel—clean uniforms and vehicles filled with gas—are now in the field. The officers notify dispatch they are available for calls. They are "10-8," a common expression meaning "in service" or ready and available. A call sign of Patrol 6, Unit 4, or Traffic Motorcycle 7 is often abbreviated or phonetically identified as Paul 6, Day 4, or Mary 7.

Communications personnel will monitor their activity and welfare now for the next eight, ten, or twelve hours.

Hidden quite often from many at the department — often the entire patrol shift and communications — and the public as well, are special units. These units include surveillance teams, undercover officers assigned to narcotics street teams, and gang units focused on street, prison, and outlaw motorcycle gangs, auto theft rings, and professional criminal "crews." Crews commit many of the more highly publicized crimes, like the jewelry heists reported on the evening news, or a bank robbery by multiple suspects with sophisticated weapons and communications equipment. The latter may plan an operation over months and are often "found out" because of their association with other career criminals.

The special units are searching, researching, watching, listening for, and desperately want, the big guys. At this writing, El Chapo, of Mexican Cartel fame, has again been taken into custody. It is major offenders like him that these units are after.

Team UC-1 is operating today, looking for a major player. Alejandro Pedro Sanchez is a POI (Person of Interest). He is also known by the nickname "Big Homes." Police call this type of nickname a moniker. As you will soon see, we're not talking about a large house or a housing development of large scale homes. We're talking about a 35 year-old gang member of 23 years. His intimate membership in Southside Varrio Locos, the SVLs, is almost legendary. Our guy is seriously overweight, 310 pounds, 5'8" with two stars burned under his left eye and a large tattoo on his back of a '33 Chevrolet Coupe, chopped and channeled (customized).

Big Homes is out on parole from a state prison, and is known to associate with both other street gang members that are "okay" with the SVLs, meaning they get along, and a motorcycle gang, the Satan Slaves. The purpose of his association with these criminal groups is primarily to make money. Sanchez has a contact who can get his hands on military weapons. He also has a contact who can provide major quantities of dope. This information has come to my attention through one of my reliable, court-tested and vetted informants.

So we will be "on the glass" or "glassing" Big Homes by videotaping, looking through high resolution telescopes, binoculars and monoculars. We may even contact NASA (National Aeronautics and Space Administration) through channels and get a peek from way up high on Big Homes when he goes to visit a friend in the middle of an orange orchard in the south central part of sunny California. We will watch him make contact with other crime types like himself—those he met in county jail or state prison or just some of his pathetic fellow homies.

22

Sanchez has earned his seamy reputation. He's been convicted of carrying a concealed weapon, home invasion, armed robbery, twice for sales of controlled substances, receiving stolen property, aggravated assault, and numerous other minor crimes. He has been arrested eighteen times. He has been found guilty sixteen times. Twice, major violations have been changed to minor violations.

He has, according to the gang code, earned respect. He has "street cred" (credibility). He carries weight in the neighborhood he's from (no pun intended). His fellow gang members will furnish him with alcohol, guns, dope, girlfriends, transportation, and living quarters, and do errands for him.

Further, he has ties to a large statewide criminal enterprise, a national criminal organization with direct linkage to South America, and even has had associations with one bona fide terrorist organization from Columbia, South America.

Mr. Sanchez is a very dangerous individual. We will watch him. He'll slip up. We'll slip in. The handcuffs will be slipped on, and UC-1 will have apprehended a major offender.

UC-1, known as Umbrella-1, gets a gold star. The unit gets its operational direction from me. My call sign is Decoy 24. I've run this unit from its inception. I've been undercover for 4½ years. We'll talk more about other operations as you read further. "On Channel, Tac-4" (tactical channel 4 is a dedicated radio frequency only for tactical operations for Umbrella-1.) Decoy 24, click, click. (Click, click means transmissions complete.)

Chapter 2
Gone Fishin' at Southfork

"Com. (communications) Center, Decoy 24."

"Go ahead, 24."

There's a slight pause with static, then a clear transmission is made.

"Com., please on Tactical Channel 2, have the watch Commander contact me. I'm 10-22 (at my location) at the Campground."

"10-4, 24."

"Thanks, 24 out."

From the Watch Commander in a very few minutes: "24, this is L-T 6 or Lima 6." (L-T is an abbreviation for lieutenant and Lima is phonetic for lieutenant.6 completes his call sign.) I respond: "Sir, please contact State Police, Major Crimes Unit, Sgt. O'Malley. He's waiting for your confirmation of my 22. He can contact me on cold cell,

'Prairie Dog.'" (A cold cell has a number not listed as a phone belonging to Decoy 24 or any police agency; but, rather, it's a "burner phone" or phone of no value that you could literally toss without consequence.)

"Ask the Sgt. to contact me this afternoon."

"Roger that, 24. Be safe; have a nice picnic!"

"Thanks, sir." (Click, click). Disconnected.

The idea of discipline, acknowledgement of rank, professional courtesy, and common sense catches my fancy. If you are senior to me, I will let you know it. Society, and even those in both law enforcement and military ranks, too often show a dismissive or cavalier attitude toward the chain of command and recognizing rank.

As I pull into the campground, I'm greeted by a campground ranger. "Good afternoon," he says. I reply, "Same to you."

"Do you have a reservation?"

"Sure do." I hand him an envelope.

As he inspects the documents he replies, "You're in Space #38, sir."

"That little 15-foot Aljo camping trailer will fit in there nicely," I say to myself. "Thank you," I say to the ranger. He waves and tells me to enjoy my stay.

So with my visitor's packet, window sticker, and campground map in hand, I drive down to Space #38.

You might be perplexed as to why I am pulling this little camping trailer. My immediate answer is, "blending." Blending is a law enforcement technique of making yourself inconspicuous. If I pull up in a 30-foot, $100,000 motor home, or a mobile command post with big letters that say, "Police Operation Command Vehicle," I might draw some attention, right? There you go! So the camping trailer does just fine.

Inside the trailer are the typical items that nearly every camper might have: potato chips, pretzels, a large can of peanuts, a loaf of white bread, peanut butter and grape jelly, two cans of pork and beans, some beef jerky, and an ice chest containing bologna, Swiss cheese, coffee creamer, some soda pop, a six-pack of beer, some ketchup, mustard, and pickle relish. In a smaller ice chest are hamburger patties, hot dogs, and some kielbasa rings. In a paper bag under the little dining table are hot dog and hamburger buns, 12-oz. drinking cups, two ceramic coffee mugs, some sugar packets, a jar of instant coffee, and plastic knives, forks, and spoons. I have a couple rolls of paper towels as well.

In campsite #40 are my unsuspecting suspects. (Isn't it odd that no one will secure campsite #39? Maybe so I can do some "glassing" of campsite #40.)

They are members of the "Devil's Demons," another troublesome outlaw motorcycle (MC) gang. This gang, like the Mongols, Hells Angels, Pagans, Outlaws, Bandidos, Satan Slaves, and so on, are typically in the illicit drug trade business. They do other types of crime as well, but all MC gangs are involved in unlawful activity that has its roots in narcotics. If they don't manufacture their own product, they outsource from a "cooker," many times an independent guy who produces their version of quality dope for them to broker.

On many an occasion, these bikers make connections directly to Mexico and acquire their supply of whatever. They also have an interest in party drugs like Ecstasy. Most of the Ecstasy is produced out of country. Southeast Asia, China, and even a few European nations manufacture party drugs. If it's "synthetic dope," man-made stuff, it's not just simply dangerous. It can be deathly dangerous.

The Demons will turn their campground into a sort of Satan's Sandbox play area — lots of partying, noise, dope-smoking, beer-guzzling, sex-carousing, and profanity-hollering. They'll disrupt family campers, intimidate campground managers, litter the area they are in, and just be the pests and criminals they are.

As they are glassed by me, my two counterparts from State Police arrive. They, too, will be paying particular attention to our neighbors. License plates get run on autos, motorcycles, trucks, whatever, and video will be taken. Their trash will eventually be sifted through and their DNA might even be taken off their beer cans or plastic glasses. We'll have photo IDs and, if we're lucky, we'll find a weak link, a possible snitch: a "rat," a person amenable to being a reliable informant.

On day three, I do down to the Southfork of the river, just about half a mile from Chimney Rock (the rock, of course, looks like a chimney). One of the bikers, a guy called "Twisted" is there. A moniker or nickname usually is related to some physical characteristic. This guy fell off his bike while lane splitting—that is, driving between cars on the freeway, straddling the painted lanes. He struck one vehicle, fell, got run over by another vehicle, got his bike totaled, and today he has a very defined limp. His hips are crooked and his head doesn't exactly sit properly about his shoulders.

At any rate, Twisted, whose driver's license name is Johnathan Nathaniel Eggelson, and I strike up a conversation. Whaddayaknow … Twisted has an outstanding felony warrant, is on probation, and hasn't the brains God gave a goose (my apologies to the reader if you are a goose lover. I know I just love a cooked goose myself).

So after I actually cast my super-duper lure a few times, and hook into a nice little rainbow trout, I watch Twisted watching me watching him. I yell, "You a fisherman?" He yells back, "No."

I tell him to come over and we warm up to one another. After maybe an hour or so, he'll take a leak in the Southfork downstream from where I'm fishing. I'll tell him to stop over for a beer at my trailer if he likes — and he likes!

And so, eventually, Twisted sings like a bird, or goose, if you will. He tells my State Trooper buddies his sad story and many tales about dope, stolen cars, and some random burglaries. Additional personnel are called from two little mountain towns — six uniformed State Troopers working the interstate and three DEA agents all assist.

Campsite #40 is today available for occupancy.

Twisted is sentenced to 180 days in county jail, while his friends are all sentenced to state prison — one for eleven years and the other two for twenty-five to life. In addition to seizing adequate quantities of dope, we seized one fully automatic AK-47, one fully automatic AR-15, and two handguns, both untraceable because of missing serial numbers. Handguns are not normally illegal; however, with serial numbers filed off, they are.

As I thank my colleagues from various agencies for their assistance and drive off from the campsite, I'm reminded of the many times my father and I went trout fishing. No kidding, on the Southfork, just below Chimney Rock. "I'm thinking good thoughts about you, Dad."

I carefully enter the freeway.

"Command Center, Decoy 24."

"Go ahead, 24."

"Suspects in custody. Caught two trout, and four bad guys."

"Well, aren't you just Field and Stream," says L-T 6 as he comes on the air.

"Yes, sir, I suppose so."

"If you're done with your picnic, you are administratively off tomorrow. So get home and I'll talk with you Friday."

"Yes, sir. 10-4. Decoy's off the air, Prairie Dog, Com. only." "Prairie Dog, Com. only" means I am now only available on cell phone.

Chapter 3
An Invitation to a Fly Race

Fyodor Dostoyevsky, a Russian author and philosopher, once said in his book *The House of the Dead* (1860-1862): "The degree of civilization in a society can be judged by entering its prisons."

Based on this notion, I can attest to the fact that we are apparently not a civilized society. I'd like to invite you to a fly race. You be the judge — civilized or uncivilized?

Often times, but not really frequently, law enforcement investigators may find it necessary to visit a state or federal prison to assist in an ongoing investigation. This was the case with one of my investigations.

I had acquired information that I needed to corroborate and my best source was presently incarcerated in prison. No doubt you may have seen an episode of *NYPD Blue* with Andy Sipowicz, where one of his many partners might need to visit the Tombs (the city's lockup), Rikers Island, a state prison on the outskirts of New York City, or Ossining, New York, site of the original Sing Sing prison.

My investigation takes me to a correctional institution which is described as a maximum security institution. I'm not a penologist but basically, here you do not have the privileges accorded medium and minimum security prisoners. You are not free to roam around, go out and spend significant time on an exercise yard, at a gymnasium — on and on. Your movements are constantly monitored by electronic means and correctional officers are strategically placed throughout the facility.

There are, however, some cracks in the wall, some breaches in security, even some people who will look the other way, to allow for indiscretions to occur. "An invitation to a fly race" would fall in that category, but far worse.

Upon arrival at this prison, which was pre-arranged and authorized, appropriate credentials are presented — executive prison personnel are informed. Consent is granted and you go from the outside to the inside. A very eerie feeling!

The individual I'm going to be interviewing is finishing a five-year sentence, reduced for a host of reasons to three years and four months. You have heard of time served in a county facility, also reduction in sentence earned for good behavior (*really?*), and for complying with your program — that means pretty much behaving yourself and attempting to better yourself. Make yourself available for counseling, enter a drug abuse prevention program, attend religious services, wear a clean prison uniform, and don't be profane or confrontational.

So … my guy is doing what he can to get out. Oddly enough, my interview will get him a reduction in his sentence and a transfer to a medium security facility. He'll also clear his conscience a bit and have a good cry, but he will also startle me with his story. To this day, when I see a fly, I shake my head and reflect quietly on the fly race.

Once an interview room has been obtained and the convict has been informed he has a visitor, he will be escorted to the interview area. He may tell his fellow convicts he's going to see his shrink, his psychologist, or his medical doctor for his headaches, but he will not tell any of his prison buddies, homies, or cronies he's going to talk with the Man. That would be me, Decoy 24.

Once he is comfortably seated, the introduction is made. "I am Detective Sam Taylor, Mr. Hagan." A handshake is extended and then the interview begins.

After not more than a twenty minute period, Mr. Hagan says he needs a break. He needs a recess. "I need to clear my head," he says. Then spontaneously he says, "I didn't have anything to do with it." I say, "What?" He snorts, "Don't con me, man. I know what's up!"

I usually think I do know what's up—but not today, not at 10:15 a.m. on a Wednesday morning, right here talking to Mr. Hagan. My tone changes slightly, almost in a patronizing manner. "I don't want you upset, I don't want you tearful; I am not here to upset you. I'm here to ask you some questions pertaining to an investigation. If there is something you would like to say which could prove helpful to both of us, I'm listening. There is no need to be fearful and it is not my intention to upset you. Do you prefer my questions, or would you prefer to just talk? You can tell me 'what's up' and I'll just listen if you like."

After some eye-wandering and staring at the tile floor, Mr. Hagan says, "Okay, man! So this is what happened…" He then proceeds to talk about an incident that has no bearing on my case. It is, however, one of the most graphic and startling stories in my storied law enforcement career. It's now time to get your fly swatter ready.

So, Mr. Hagan begins: "I was supposed to clean all the floor drains in the kitchen area according to Cook Sanderson. He said, 'After you do your degreasing of all the floors, mop them with floor sanitizer, put the floor fans on them, then go back by the walk-in refrigerator and the freezer. Open up that chemical closet, get out the enzyme cleaner, and put one cup in a bucket. Add a gallon of hot water to the bucket, then pour it in each drain. You got five drains, so five buckets of enzyme cleaner.' Got it?

"So I do the first drain by the eating tables, then I do another bucket by the eating tables, then I move into the kitchen area and to the drain under the multi-sink area, then to the floor drain by the food preparation tables then the last one by the hot water heater, back by the walk-ins and the dry goods. I'm telling you, man, I didn't know about no fly race. I don't care what anybody says. I don't go for NO fly races, *honest.*"

At this point, I have no idea what he's talking about. I do know that he's hiding something. I also have no idea how floor drain cleaning has anything to do with my visit.

"Let's continue, Mr. Hagan. At least we're talking, and I thank you very much for opening up. Do you feel like there is more you would like to tell me?"

"Yeah," he says, "but I'm not involved—no way. You got it?"

I sit quietly and assure him, "I got it." So he says, "As soon as that 'meat' come in the cafeteria, I know it was trouble." ("Meat," or sometimes "new resident", is often used to refer to a new prisoner.)

"That guy called Handyman says, 'Come on over, boy, what's your name?' He tells him, 'Kenneth.' Handyman says, 'Kenneth, what do you want in the cafeteria?' Kenneth says, 'Guard Jones told me to go to the cafeteria and ask for spices. He said get some salt and pepper there, and probably a stick or two of butter. Then he started laughing, really laughing.' So, Handyman says, 'Son, you want to meet a couple guys back here, why I'll get you what you need.'

"'Okay,' says this damn fool, Kenneth. 'This is "Doo"; he always keeps his hair slicked with a nylon over it, and Miller Lite 'cause this fool loves to drink Miller Lite. They call me Handyman 'cause I'm creative with tools and such.' Kenneth says 'Hi' to Doo and Miller Lite. Then Doo says, 'You play cards?' Ken says, 'No' and Doo says, 'How about races? You like horse races like the Kentucky Derby?' Ken says he likes horses, not any horse racing. Oh, God! Now it's gonna get real bad!

"I'm really quiet by the walk-ins and the hot water heater. No one can see me, and they can't hear, either. No way anybody knew I was there. How the hell did you know? I want to know, how did you know?"

"Don't get upset, Mr. Hagan, it's not about you," I tell him. "You're hidden, right?" "Yeah," he says. "So go ahead with your story."

"'Well,' Doo says, 'go over there by the sinks and we'll show you this fun game we play—it's like horse racin.' So Kenneth goes over by the sinks. I think that's when Miller Lite goes out to the dumpster to catch some flies. I know

Handyman is probably going to get a couple towels to gag Kenneth so he can't scream.

"Doo says, 'You got some flies?' And Miller Lite says, 'Yeah, four good ones.' Doo pulled off their wings, I know he did and put 'em on the floor. Handyman says, 'Pick a fly to win the race.' Kenneth says, 'What race?' Handyman says, 'The Fly Race.' Kenneth says, 'I never heard of this, but I pick the little green fly.' Miller Lite says, 'First fly to walk under the sink below the tile line, you know, right here — wins.' It's over for Kenneth now! I hear Handyman say, 'Your fly seems to be winnin'!' Then I hear a boot stomp. Kenneth says, 'Hey, why did you kill my fly?' Then I hear a struggle — I hear muffled yelling, 'Who's first?'

"Handyman says, 'Doo, you first, then Miller Lite, then me. Drag him over to the flour sacks. Get his pants off. You want a stick of butter or some vegetable oil?' Doo says, 'Grease him up with butter.' Then muffled screams. Then more screams when Miller Lite starts sayin', 'How about it Kenneth? You never will come to this cafeteria again.' He laughs. The Handyman also rapes him, I think. I couldn't see nothin'. Only silhouettes of them movin' around through a polished aluminum refrigerator door.

"When it's all over, they all leave and Kenneth is out cold. So I run to the fire alarm, pull it, and run. That's all I know. But I do know that that kid, Kenneth, jumped from the third tier with his hands tied behind his back, headfirst, 'cause he couldn't stand being punked out." He pauses and says to me, "How did you know, man, how did you know?"

I say to Mr. Hagan, "Thank you—you've been very helpful." I push a call button, and officers come and return him to his cell.

Within a matter of minutes I'm in the Associate Warden's office, explaining the story. He remarks, "How did you know?" then laughs. "Glad you talked to one of our inmates. I'll get a couple of investigators in to interview you."

I explain as politely as possible, "Sir, I am here as a police investigator, assigned undercover, and it is not in my best interests to agree to any interviews. Might you be kind enough to call my supervisor, J. D. Taylor? He is the Commander of the Statewide Intelligence Task Force, to which I'm assigned."

The Warden remarks, "J. D. Taylor and I are close friends; he helped me out about two years ago on two separate Aryan Warriors cases. He had some investigator assigned then who was deep into the Aryan Syndicate. All I know is all the documents I was given to read were signed by an investigator he said was the best."

"Well," I said, "I'm glad to hear you know him. Please call him and, if I may, I need to get out of prison."

We both had a quick laugh then he walked me to his office door. "Detective, I think the fellow's reports were all signed Decoy 24. Ever heard anything like that?"

I smiled and remarked, "No, sir, can't say a thing about Decoy 24."

As I left the prison grounds, my radio crackles, "Decoy 24."

"Go ahead, Com."

"Please contact Commander Taylor ASAP, 'says he needs to talk to you."

"10-4, Decoy 24." Click, click.

Summary: The three perps in the prison case were all found guilty of assault to commit great bodily harm, sex crimes violations, and involuntary manslaughter under threat. They all remain in custody for life at different facilities.

Guard Jones was found complicit of this and other crimes; he was investigated by the Department of Corrections Internal Affairs Unit, relieved of duty, found guilty of numerous offenses, and he is presently serving a 35-year sentence in a state prison located in the southern region of the USA. Because he was a prison guard, he is in protective custody. Each day he spends 22½ hours under lock and key with only 90 minutes for exercise which is done on a roof by himself and observed by two correctional officers, no doubt. "Don't cotton much with his behavior."

Chapter 4
Don't Wear a Trench Coat in the Summer

Common sense would dictate that when it's 95 degrees out, it would be an excellent idea not to wear a trench coat. Also, a trench coat worn in the summertime might lead a patrol officer or an investigator to believe you might be wearing a "shoulder-rig" just underneath that coat.

I'm working in tandem with three other agencies, attempting to interrupt daytime armed robberies by street thugs. I'm spending most of my time, due to my long hair and long beard, along with my filthy clothing, *blending* with the homeless.

Two things will come out of this assignment. Number one: three suspects will be taken into custody, charged and convicted. Number two: I might very well have taken on volunteering at a food bank some years ago, and still do today, because of the experience of associating with the homeless.

Com: "Decoy 24." "Go ahead, 24."

"I'll be working for the next four days out of jurisdiction. Please contact Commander J. D. Taylor if I am needed. He will make contact on a secure portable (secure portable phone). Please note, an email has been forwarded to all Watch Commanders, and Lt. Sherman at SIU."

"10-4, 24. Take care." Click, click.

While I am associated with a large and underserved homeless population, I am utterly amazed at the number of homeless veterans. I am a Vietnam veteran, and have true compassion for my fellow servicemen and women. There is a disproportionate number of vets that are drug-addicted as well; the stink of human excrement at night, urine, vomit, empty liquor bottles, and used syringes is almost overwhelming.

Day One: I leave my homeless community around 8:00 p.m. From that time forward, I walk about fifteen blocks away from my AOR (area of responsibility). I enter the hotel from the rear kitchen door, "show my tin" and take a laundry elevator to the 4th floor, lay out my stinking clothes, shower, call my wife, watch a ball game, order room service, and crash. The reason I stay a bit later in an AOR is to learn some names of people. If, after that, they recognize me and I have two or three dollars, maybe I'll get some fast food to pass on. Then, we have a relationship. I call it *blending*.

Day Two and Three are uneventful.

On Day Four, about 11:15 a.m., it's time to go tactical. Three individuals pull up in a loading zone in a late model Ford E-150 van. A van was noted in earlier briefings by the L. E. (law enforcement) community as a possible getaway vehicle — light color paint: white, tan, or, for me, how about a faded yellow.

As the driver exits the van, he puts on sunglasses, also noted from briefing "hot sheets." The passenger gets out with a black ball cap on and also puts on sunglasses. The dude in the back of the van gets out of the sliding door with a trench coat on, wearing a droopy hat. He saunters over to the corner and leans against a building.

I'm not the only game in town, however — two other officers are sitting in a Molly-Moo dairy truck and another officer sits inside a taxicab. Two additional officers are inside a pharmacy with a coffee shop. They are in sportswear and look like casual guys, not the po-po. They drink coffee and chat.

I hear over my ear piece, which I just inserted from the OIC (Officer In Charge) in the delivery truck, "These are our guys, I believe. Use extreme caution."

I will discuss the takedown procedure, but let us continue with the excitement. Did I share with you my position? I'm literally two homeless people away from the trench coat man. I don't know one of the two homeless, but because of my having been in that neighborhood, I do know the other guy. His name is Herman and he's a homeless man who used to sell cars. He's single, a heavy drinker, and an ex-soldier who did one tour in Desert Storm in the early 1990s. I tell him I want to rest a little, then go to St. Francis of Assisi Soup Kitchen for some lunch. (I ate at homeless shelters and soup kitchens during the day. Remember, *blending*.)

So, I am about twelve feet from Trench Coat. I carry a .45 caliber 1911, and small .380 for street work. They are concealable, comfortable, and, with a great deal of perfect practice, accurate! Practice does not make perfect. Perfect practice makes perfect.

Shooting with two hands, shooting with one hand, shooting with your weak hand, shooting in the dark, shooting laying on your right side, shooting laying on your left side — it all requires perseverance and dedication.

I dedicate all my attention to Trench Coat — and particularly a crease in the trench coat that starts around the right armpit area and goes down to just below the pocket of his sagging blue jeans. It's definitely a shoulder-rig. If I physically tackle him about the waist, he can't raise his weapon. If I force him or order him onto the sidewalk, on his stomach, he'll be laying on the weapon. If I can grab a right hand or right arm, he can't raise or operate the weapon.

As I watch him and glance to my left, both sets of sunglasses enter the large liquor store. It's open 24 hours a day and has money pickups at noon and 6:00 p.m. The armored vehicle will be here in about ten minutes if it's on schedule. All the intelligence gained and passed on the surveillance/takedown team is helpful. There are two unanswered questions:

1. Are there more guys in a layoff vehicle just waiting?
2. Do they want to take the armored car rather than the store?

Sweat streams down Trench Coat's face as he leans against the building in the noonday sun. The bad guys—on the run. The officer in the taxi orders them, "Police! Stop or I'll shoot!" They don't stop; he doesn't shoot. Too many people in the area.

I have to decide: should I pull my weapon, jump the suspect, tackle him and, of course in each case, maybe get shot by a pair of sunglasses? I hear, "Get in, man…" as the two sunglasses jump into the van. It starts up. Trench Coat starts to go for the sliding door. I trip him—not something taught in the academy back in the day—but Trench Coat goes down. I jump on him, roll him over, place the .380 gently against his temple, and announce, "Police! Do not resist or I'll shoot you. You got it?"

"I got it!"

The sunglasses take off through the intersection and are pursued by two marked cars. The taxicab flips a U-turn and joins the pursuit. Both officers in the delivery truck run over to me and while one has the suspect at gunpoint, the other cuffs him. I gently and safely holster my weapon. One of the officers says, "We got one of them! They'll get the others in the pursuit."

A voice from the sidewalk, leaning up against the wall, says, "I knew you weren't 'on the street.'" It was Herman. I smile and say, "What makes you say that?" He replies, "'Cause your clothes are dirty but you smell like bath soap every morning. I never see you goin' to the Y for a shower..." "So, you know!"

I guess my *blending* is slippin'. Can't smell like a cupcake or Irish Spring® and not have somebody wondering.

I shake Herman's hand, tell him I won't be back tomorrow. I pull out my wallet, take out a $20 bill, and hand it to him. He looks at me and says, "Thanks, man. Oh, and by the way, you got a name?"

I smile back and say, "Yeah, Decoy 24, but you can call me Sam." Herman laughs, "Nice meeting you, Sam." I say, "Same here. See ya."

As I walk off to go to a predetermined area station to file my report, I'm filled with emotions: Trench Coat looked about sixteen. Herman's going to be on the street. I'm thinkin', "What exactly caused me to trip the perp? That was a great move, if I do say so myself!"

I chuckle and keep walking to the destination I've been given earlier. Just then I see one of the two plain clothes guys in an unmarked unit. He yells out the passenger window, "All suspects in custody. No shots fired." I smile and nod. He says, "Want to ride?" I say, "No, thanks, I'm enjoying the walk." He replies, "Okay, see you at the station," and he gives me a slight hand wave.

A homeless guy leaning on the building next to me flips the plain clothes officer the "bird" and says, "Plain clothes, punk-ass police." I look at him and do the same, finger high in the air, and say back, "Nothin' but a punk!" Blending, remember.

Summary: All three suspects were found guilty of armed robbery. Both pair of sunglasses go to State Prison, seven to twenty years. Trench Coat goes to a juvenile facility for eighteen months.

Chapter 5
Even Grandpa Smoked Dope

When working certain types of cases, the importance of kinship and friendship should not be overlooked. There's something to be said about the saying that, "the fruit doesn't fall far from the tree!"

Kinship displayed itself brutally in the winter of 2015 in San Bernardino, California with a terrorist attack being conducted by a husband and wife team. It reminded me of a husband and wife team that were on a crime spree, active in the 1970s: Emily and Bill Harris of the SLA (Symbionese Liberation Army).

The summer of 2016 would be marred by the Orlando, Florida shooting at a nightclub called Pulse. The male shooter had confided in his wife that he was planning criminal activities, if initially only by threat. Kinship and criminality didn't end with the demise of Bonnie and Clyde nearly one hundred years ago.

Friendship plays a role as well. The Al Qaeda hijackers of 2001 had maintained a very strong friendship amongst themselves. In San Diego, California they took flying lessons together. There were trips to a local mosque by many of them. They roomed together in the same apartment and socialized in the evenings and on weekends together. The point is, consider friendship along with kinship.

Remember Klebold and Harris, the teenage attackers at Columbine High School in 1999 in Littleton, Colorado? This duo of very close friends planned their fierce attack and carried it out after planning and practicing for months. Point of fact: close, close friends.

Although not a member of any Colorado law enforcement agency, I did do an exhaustive case study of this incident. I visited the site, interviewed officers, and, after completing a "lessons-learned" analysis, presented my findings at a number of seminars provided throughout the country. Today, many of those "lessons-learned" continue to be part of law enforcement training curricula nationwide.

There was also a close relationship kept by the two associates who conducted the armed robbery at a Bank of America in North Hollywood, California in 1997. These two men developed a friendship after working out together on numerous occasions at a gym. They also obtained a safe house in a smaller city bordering Los Angeles where the two could hide out.

Never underestimate the importance of kinship and friendship in cases involving multiple suspects, criminal syndicates, and street, biker and prison gangs.

The circumstances involving Grandpa and the grandsons not only address kinship but their production and sale of illicit drugs. We're not talking about tunnels under an international port of entry, nor are we interested in observing Panga boats being beached on the coastal shores.

This time it's precursor drugs and "finished product." The raw goods for manufacturing ready-to-sell drugs are stored in an outbuilding next to a small ranch house in the middle of a very large orchard of orange and avocado trees. So, we have a family in "the major quantity sale of dope" business.

Grandpa has been doing an excellent job of blending himself. He portrays a fruit and vegetable stand employee with his straw hat, raggedy light blue work shirt, old jeans, and a neckerchief sometimes worn around his neck. If the neckerchief is on, the store's open. If the neckerchief is off, the store's closed. Of course, there is no store.

His grandsons can see him through binoculars and when he is not wearing the neckerchief they exercise extreme caution. The neckerchief came off on one occasion when an unfamiliar pickup truck came down a dirt road toward the ranch house. He quickly pulled off his neckerchief, waved it in the air, and approached the truck. The driver inside asked for directions to a nursery not far up the road. The old man assured the confused driver it was just up the road on the left about four miles. The driver thanked him for his help and turned around and bounced on the dirt road back to the paved highway. That allegedly confused and lost driver was actually an undercover officer. His call sign: Decoy 24.

In cases like this, law enforcement does well to lose the Ford 4-door sedans, the Ford Explorers, and frankly anything with three or four aerials on it and emergency lights hidden in the front grill. The vehicles of choice for this operation: the old pickup truck, a brown step van delivery truck, a Weber step van bread truck, and a two-ton spraying truck borrowed from the Department of Agriculture. These trucks are common in agricultural areas, spraying for fruit flies, mosquitoes, and other pests. Finally, a Polaris off-road vehicle; it sits two with a small bed behind the passengers. It will be a great vehicle to go in between the trees if the suspects jump on their ATVs.

So, we're blending, using equipment designed for the task, and now it's time to do tactical reconnaissance. We will do overhead surveillance with a bi-plane usually used for crop dusting. The owner of a crop dusting service will do a couple of fly-overs to acquaint one of the team members with the terrain.

I've bought dope out of a window of a VW Bug! When all-night surveillance was required, it was done from an old camper shell placed on top of an old Toyota-100 light truck. When drive-by surveillance was required, on one occasion an ice cream truck was used — once down the street with the irritating chimes and bells, then once again without the noise.

There was even one operation where a cement truck was used in an upscale suburban neighborhood. While the driver of the cement truck surveyed where he might pour, the second operator got out and pretended to measure an area of sidewalk as though it was a repair pour. The area measured was in front of two houses. One house was unimportant; the other was the target house for a next day, early morning raid. We often joked, calling those operations "Sunrise Service." Best time to serve arrest and search warrants? 5:30 a.m. to 6:00 a.m.

When doing tactical recon, you're looking for hazards, positions of cover, the actual approach to a given building, the entry point to gain access to the building, fences that might need to be scaled or defeated, locks on doors, and so forth. This information is discussed at a pre-RAID briefing. Many times, the acronym RAID actually defined the briefing.

RAID meant:
- R: Reconnaissance
- A: Assault plan
- I: Intelligence Information gathered (i.e., number of suspects, presumed-armed, dogs or other animals—a sort of "Who's who in the zoo" type thing)
- D: Directed Deployment Strategy, meaning, which officers go where and do what.

I suppose if you're really pouring concrete, it might mean:

- R: Raise gutter slide or chute.
- A: Activate the pour switch.
- I: Indicate with a closed fist for somebody to stop the flow of cement.
- D: Drive away in the truck after pouring the cement then wash down the chute with water.

You get the point. I don't know anything about pouring concrete, but I am familiar with tactical operations. I'm dialed up: sophisticated blending, observational skills, an accurate recon plan. All these elements when in place allow for a smooth operation and safety to all law enforcement personnel.

Other points not discussed herein would include personnel and equipment, their positions, the actual entry technique be it a ram or explosive entry, and suspect take-down tactics.

To continue: always, always "blending." Grandpa is not the only clever one — he blends — so do we.

In this particular instance, Grandpa, the lookout, played the fool. When the ranch house and corrugated aluminum building next to it got hit by a high precision assault team, he acted the part. He, too, had rehearsed what he was told: "Viejo, don't get nervous. Just don't speak. Act really frightened, okay?" Grandpa: "No problem!"

But once Grandpa was informed he, too, would go to jail for dope, his tune changed and he sang like a bird. He identified his grandsons, where shipments of precursor chemicals came from, who the grandsons' associates were, and a significant list of customers. Not a criminal cartel, but it was "all in the family."

As the title states, "Even Grandpa Smoked Dope," Grandpa did have some high grade weed. "Personal use stuff," he said. If he smoked a little weed, then he was comfortable just sitting around the ranch house or out on the road.

He had a small fruit stand where he sold oranges and avocados. A little pocket change … and blending. He looked like a roadside vendor, alright.

Summary: Remember, kinship and friendship. Grandpa turned state's evidence. He explained how the grandsons built the indoor grow house and sold their merchandise. He explained how certain chemicals were mixed with normal air via a large evaporation cooler and thereby cut down on the chemical smell that was released into the environment. Grandpa did a little stint in an honor camp—fourteen months or so. The grandsons receive major sentences to state prisons.

Grandpa's name was Joaquin—that's Jack. I sort of thought the honor farm should have given him a little piece of land with a couple of avocado trees and called it, "Happy Jack's Avocado Ranch." I'm certain of one thing: Grandpa and the grandsons probably have a strained relationship now. So much for kinship.

Decoy 24, out.

Chapter 6
Buy-Walk, Buy-Bust, Bye-Bye!

Quick definitions:

Buy-Walk—the dope is scored (bought), or the stolen property or the illegal firearms purchased, and the officer or officers walk away and do not immediately initiate an arrest. The officer may be building a more sophisticated case, gain trust with the seller for continued or larger buys, or simply authenticate they are not law enforcement.

My initial operations in an undercover capacity were primarily "buy-walks," to not mark me as a cop. Once it's established, "I'm not a cop!", some serious police work can begin. Didn't I mention who I am? I'm Decoy 24—I am the police.

Buy-Bust—the arrest after the sales transaction is virtually immediate. Example: An officer makes a street buy from the driver of a vehicle. The driver hands over the dope, gets the money, and attempts to drive off. A group of police vehicles—primarily unmarked but with a few marked— collapse on him. He is effectively blocked in and numerous officers in identifiable police garb—windbreakers that say "Police", vests that are marked "Police" or "Sheriff" or "State Police" or whatever—run up on the driver.

They yell, "Police!", show badges, and as they run up on the driver, do a quick visual search of the interior of the vehicle for weapons, of course. These officers are called the arrest team.

If undercover officers are being deployed, recognition or familiarity usually occurs at a briefing prior to field operations. (UC officers, remember, have blended in with the neighborhood.) Departmental shooting policy would be reviewed, as well as a reminder about fire discipline and overall use of force.

I have been the recipient of undisciplined use of force. I have personally had weapons drawn on me, without provocation. I have been cornered and stepped on by police horses, known as mounted units. I have been run into by motorcycle officers while attempting to conduct an operation. I have also been thrown to the ground, punched, and handcuffed, only later to be issued an apology. "Sorry, man, I didn't know you were one of us, or a cop..." or whatever. The officers pay a UC officer a compliment when the UC officer is a victim of operational blending.

Once in New York, a look-alike rabbi intervened during an arrest. Another NYPD officer confronted the rabbi and said, "Rabbi, calm down. You don't want to be arrested." He looked at the officer and said, very quietly, "I'm on the job, his precinct, and take it easy on him, the arrestee — he's my informant." The quick response, a grin, a head shake, and, "Okay, got it." A more gentle arrest was made — and, of course, the rabbi meets his informant later at the station house.

To change things up a bit, sometimes a vehicle (cold-plated, meaning not registered to any one individual, but an undercover vehicle) may drive along a street where sidewalk dealers are located. The officer driving the car makes their buy and, with the drugs or other contraband in their possession, they drive away.

Officers stationed in strategic positions actually watch the transaction. As the officer drives away, he puts his hand up to rub his forehead — or raises a ball cap off his head then puts it back on.

At "the sign," officers know an arrest can be made, now or in the not-too-distant future. When the arrest is made it's now *Bye-Bye!* Into a marked car or other transportation vehicle, the suspects go to booking or processing as the case may be.

Then there are situations where the buy plan has a glitch. Here's an example: The officer is fitted with an electronic device. The officer who has had previous contact with the seller or dealers goes to, say, their house. The undercover officer enters the house and officers outside rely on audio to authenticate the buy. There may be a verbal sign like, "Sure is good dope..." or "I'll leave out through a different door, if you don't mind." The verbal sign confirms the buy and an arrest team makes entry, verbally announcing, "Police! Police! Get on the floor!", and clears the entire residence while securing suspects. Every room, every closet, the attic, the cellar, the basement, the attached or unattached garage, outbuildings away from the house, like sheds, parked motorhomes, mobile homes, vehicles parked outside, even looking over the fence—the perimeter is secured, not just the inside area.

On one particular incident, the electronic device shorted out and failed. The officer finally ran out the front door yelling, "This sure is good dope" at the top of his lungs, and watched the entire entry team going in as he was running out.

This is a heady and comical situation, particularly when the inside officer might have repeated himself three or four times. Once, the dealer was said to have mentioned to the undercover buying officer, "Why do you keep saying this is sure good dope? I know it! I sell it!"

It's only as the officer runs off frantically—and entry officers are busting in aggressively—that the seller figures it out. So many of them are short on reasoning!

So you buy-walk or buy-bust and so often tell the suspect, "So long, see ya. Wouldn't want to be ya!"

I can attest to hearing many in custody saying, "Yea, but you said, 'I'm not the police. Do I look like the police?'" This is not entrapment—it's well-thought-out, disciplined police work.

Chapter 7
The War Bride's All Alone

This wedding takes the cake … and the groom, too. As two seemingly young people in love exchange vows in a community church, little do they know that the expression, "Till death do us part" will pay them a visit in under an hour.

The groom was a well-known gang banger. He was known to the police department's gang unit, the county prosecutor's office, the integrated state gang task force, the county probation department, and the county sheriff's department.

His trouble began as an elementary school student; they followed him through middle school where he was twice suspended, and onto high school where he attended for two years, only to be permanently expelled.

He was a gangster with a flair for two things: he loved tagging buildings (a street graffiti artist) and he enjoyed participating in drive-by shootings into inhabited dwellings.

He once did a drive-by with two crime partners on a rival gang member at a hospital as the rival was being taken out of a paramedic vehicle. The hospital drive-by was to avenge the failed drive-by shooting by another member of the Varrio Lomas Gang. A reputation is quickly tarnished by a failed drive-by attempt.

He also did a drive-by on a vacant house (no potential victims there) and did another shooting into the wrong house, not occupied by any rival gang member. He did shoot a 42-year-old mother of three. She survived with minor injuries. However, a gunshot wound is a gunshot wound, nonetheless. He was sent to state prison twice and paroled a few months later.

Our bride just loved her parolee husband-to-be. She was too sympathetic, too young, and too stupid to stay clear of her "gangsta." She seemed to enjoy the notoriety of hangin' with the gang. Of course, it was probably for good reason, as she was four months pregnant. Unfortunately, this relationship was, like too many gang romances, short-lived.

The Varrio Lomas (meaning, a small town nestled in some hills) homeboys make up a gang with a history that goes back 60 years or so. You can still find old men on some street corners in the seamy side of town who remember the day. Like veterans of the military, they recall their wars in the barrio with at least two other neighborhood gangs.

One old dude named Leo and I had quite a talk under a canopy that shaded a municipal transit bus line bench. He tells me, "I was down with the Lomas Vatos in the sixties and seventies. Then we stole cigarettes from little family-like stores, and soda, to make soda wine. We kicked some ass, but got our ass kicked, and sometimes, to be honest, stold (stole) a car." Of course, honesty was, I'm sure, a well-known trait of Leo.

We talked at length about how the gangs got more dangerous when some of the "Carnales" (brothers) came home from Nam. "I never went to no war. I broke my leg really bad in a car accident, so I didn't have to go."

I took the opportunity to tell him, "I did! 1967-1968, Brown Water Navy, Cua Viet River." I stared at him to make my point.

We talked about initiation into the gang, called "Jumpin' In." A quick five minute version of their boot camp: "…you get jumped by five or six bona fide members of the gang. They beat the hell out of you, then congratulate you for 'takin' the blows!' Now you're a Homeboy."

I listen intently and make some small talk. "What's in the bag, Leo?" He says, "Take a swig. It's grape soda."

"What's in the recipe?" I ask.

"Well, grape soda, Robitussin® cough syrup, and some cheap muscatel wine. I can sip this bottle all day long. I been drinkin' my grape soda wine for years."

I let my mind wander as to what would cause someone to join a gang. It's certainly the surrogate family for some, it's a badge of courage for some, and, no doubt, you bet some benefits—although illegally obtained—from membership.

I think about the apparent innocence of a can of spray paint—spraying exterior walls of buildings, parked trucks in delivery lots, even boxcars sitting in yards. Take a look at boxcars when the opportunity presents itself. You'll be hard-pressed not to find street writing.

I want to give you a quick lesson in gang graffiti. Here's an example: the Varrio Jalisco Locos, the VJLs, put their writing both within the neighborhood, like a dog peein' everywhere to mark its territory, and they also venture out of their neighborhood. When they mark up an area considered "the dirt" of a rival gang, trouble begins.

So the VJLs put their mark, their writing, on a wall of, let's say, a laundromat.

The Locos have advertised that this is their wall, and their territory, Por Vida (for life). The R means we are ruling the area.

Now the rival gang sees this writing in the neighborhood so they must react. First, cross it out with a big X, sometimes called a "Puta Mark" which tells the Locos that Varrio Lomas is in charge. You are on Lomas turf—you are whores, and so is your placa (writing).

There may even be another gang, like the Avenues, who feel that this is their turf. The Avenues control an area from 7th Avenue to 25th Avenue. The avenues run east and west, bordered by Mountain View Blvd. and Canal Street. (Canal Street is next to a large aqueduct carrying storm water, and it runs through town.)

The VJLs see their writing X'd out and it's on! What's even more perplexing, the Avenues may also mark up the graffiti that has already been scribbled on by Varrio Lomas.

If you don't have patrol officers and gang unit detectives working this graffiti you miss out on understanding that there are three gangs in the area. Also, there will very possibly be payback or a war because of all the X-ing out of one gang's mark by another gang.

The earlier marks by the Varrio Lomas also have nicknames that identify who is X-ing out. "Lil Flaco" is a moniker for a little, skinny guy in the Varrio Lomas. Big Nose is a member with a big nose. "Chiva" is a nickname for someone with mannerisms or physical characteristics of a billy goat, such as long chin hairs.

So if we are investigating this gang activity, we have three knuckleheads who have identified themselves for us. We still don't know a great deal about the players in the Avenues or the VJLs. We can bet on retaliation by one gang or another in short order.

Leo and I continue our conversation and he tells me how, when he was in "County" (county jail), the drink of choice was a concoction of canned prunes or peaches, secreted in the inmates' mouths, taken back to a cell, and spit in a can or a plastic or foam drinking glass.

Then, the inmates would go to "sick call" or "med call" and get whatever they could to mix with the fruit. It could be Geritol® and rubbing alcohol, as an example. This fruit drink was called "jail juice" or "pruno."

I visited a county honor camp to interview an individual and correctional officers told me about how certain pain relieving medications were actually shoved up the rectum, absorbed, and then the prisoner would get high. They called it a "Power Pack."

Leo and I finish our conversation when he boards the #115 Bus, going to nowhere for all I knew.

So, back to our wedding. Out of church saunter the bride and groom. He pulls his pants up high with both hands, then signals to his homeboys his gang sign with his right hand. The bride has most of her wedding gown train being held by two attendants, but she also has a large bunch of fabric held in one hand so she doesn't stumble. Down the church stairs they come … Mr. and Mrs. Gansta!

Shots ring out and stucco and wood chips bounce off the church exterior walls and window shutters. The groom falls down and so does a groomsman. Two other wedding attendees go down as well.

The rival gang, the shooters, yell out, "Avenues, Consafos." The message is: "We are who shot you and what are you going to do about it?"

Also, everyone sees a '63 Chevrolet Impala, candy apple red in color with chrome rims, oversize tires, and a spare tire kit on the rear of the vehicle.

The groom is "DATS" (Dead At The Scene). The groomsman will survive. The attendees will survive. The church will be repaired … the bride's broken heart will not.

Law enforcement authorities have more than enough to make arrests. Chico, the shooter, and Manuelito, the driver, two documented Avenues gang members, are in custody in less than 48 hours.

The Avenues will boast that the VJLs and Varrio Lomas are slippin'. There will be payback.

With hundreds of gangs making up a gang population of 700,000 to 800,000 documented gang members, the violence will continue.

There are not enough social programs, recreational programs, church-sponsored programs, specialized police gang units, or anything else, to stop the menace of gang crime.

In 1983, the problem was examined in another book I wrote, *Street Gangs*. I said then, 33 years ago, "Get a handle on it, or the gang epidemic will never be stopped." What an indictment of all those who "talked the talk" about gangs but were sadly mistaken. I still remember one chief of police telling me, in no uncertain terms, "I can't have a gang problem in this city. It'll make me and the city look bad. No gangs exist in this city. Do you understand?"

My response: "No, Chief. No, sir. I don't understand!" That city today is one of the largest cities in America … with a major gang problem.

One of my fellow operators once said, "Gangs are like cockroaches. Once you got 'em, you can't get rid of 'em."

Chapter 8
I Am 9-1-1

It's 7:15 a.m. and I'm sitting at a bus stop. There's an elderly lady sharing the bench with me. I'm glancing across the street towards a strip mall parking lot. The parking lot has two unknown, unoccupied cars in it and one step van with delivery truck markings on it. It's not a delivery truck. One of the store suites has vertical window blinds pulled shut. It's not a store suite. An apparently homeless man rifles through some trash bins that are scattered around the parking area, looking for aluminum cans. He's not a homeless man.

Without warning, a stinky young man with filthy clothes and bare feet grabs the lady's purse next to me. He struggles to rip it from her shoulder and pushes her off the bench. I didn't hear him.

This is one of those moments. Do I pursue him on foot? Do I let it happen? After all, "it's only a purse snatch." The operation this morning allows me some flexibility. So … the chase is on. Within about thirty feet or so, he's down on the sidewalk.

The inside team at the store suite has called the local police. In a matter of four or fewer minutes, two marked patrol units, light bars flickering and sirens wailing can be seen in the not-so-far distance. One unit drives over a meridian, flips a U-turn, and parks on the roadway directly next to me. The other unit coming to my assistance makes a U-turn at the intersection nearest me and pulls in behind the first patrol unit. One officer, a sergeant, gets out of his car and hustles to my aid. He opens his handcuff pouch and bends down to restrain the suspect. The other officer observes from a tactical position. The sergeant chides me with a comment, "Don't you UC guys carry cuffs? What kind of cop are you?" I smile and tell him, "We detectives let the uniforms do the real police work."

As the "perp" (perpetrator) is stowed and secured in one of the cruisers, I return to comfort the elderly lady I shared the bench with just moments earlier. She looks at me with confusion, and some amazement. "Young man," she says, "you should have called 9-1-1. That's a much safer thing to do."

I smile at her and show her my badge secured under my sock on my left ankle. "See my shield? Ma'am, I am 9-1-1."

To this day I will remember her look of amazement and the line that made me smile: "Glory be! Are you an undercover guy, like on TV?" I smile even more, "Yes, ma'am, just like on TV." The officer nearest me, the sergeant, just shakes his head in dismay and distinctly says, "Give me a break."

Outcome: Purse snatcher charged in criminal court. He receives 90 days in county jail and one year probation. The operation across the street goes on without me. Patrol personnel are 10-8 (back in service to answer calls). My "bench buddy" caught the #210 bus after refusing medical assistance. Glory be! What a sweet lady.

Chapter 9
Lookin' at You, Lookin' at Me, Lookin' at You

Good old fashioned police work is not a thing of the past! Sometimes unrelenting hard work and long hours are the recipe for success. There is a place for advanced technology and sophisticated forensic science, but like learning to hit a baseball or ride a bicycle, the basics are important.

Case in point: There's a lot to be said about police personnel that have the tools and demeanor to do certain assignments. A nervous person may not be the best pick for long term surveillance. They may be too nervous to look through a telescope for hours. They may not be the person who can sit in a vehicle for hours and hours looking through binoculars. You eat in the vehicle, urinate in the vehicle (in a bottle, not actually on the seat or carpeting), you stay awake and do not nod off. You know what to look for and you scan an area, looking for whatever it is. It may be movement in a house, comings and goings of people, or dogs on the property who can "snitch off" an approach team with their barking. All of these things become important. Are there individuals who regularly come out and do counter-surveillance looking for police? (Remember blending.) Think about how one must disguise oneself so as not to jeopardize a surveillance operation. Attention to detail, patience, and creative thinking are all important. Eyes on the situation constantly are asking, "What am I looking for?" And, "What am I looking at?"

There was an operation in the desert Southwest some years back that comes to mind. It challenged the creativity of those on the outer perimeter surveillance team. It involved a country club golf resort. The rooms to be watched were not able to be seen from a short distance. There was a pool, a swim-up bar, and an open lawn area. The OT (observation team) needed to be deployed about 60 to 70 yards away. Think about it: nearly a football field away would be the eyes of an UC operator. No closer. That distance is problematic.

The individuals being watched are notorious criminals. They are labeled "OC" (organized crime) criminals. They are part of an organized criminal syndicate. The way they behave leads to an investigation by federal authorities assisted by a joint agency task force. Under the guidelines of the federal law, the RICO Act (Racketeer Influenced and Corrupt Organizations Act), they are "big fish." Labels like "goodfellas" and "wiseguys" come to mind. You can recall movies like *The Godfather* and *The Departed*. These are the kinds of individuals that are under surveillance.

Most of the bad guys are not locals to the southwestern US. They fly in from big cities back east. There are agencies watching them leave their various cities from commercial airports. There are other agencies that follow them when they arrive at their destination airport. Other individuals will follow them to the country club. There are strategic operational plans in place upon their arrival.

Photos have been taken of them leaving from the departure city to the destination city. More photos and video as the individuals go to limousines, shuttle buses, or even those who might use rental vehicles. Keep in mind: the bad guys know they are POI's (Persons Of Interest). They know there will be some police presence somewhere. They know they are being watched. Days earlier, hotel management would have been personally visited by authorities. Also, days earlier there were telephone calls made to certain hotel management personnel. There would have been ideas regarding planting listening devices on room service carts, electronic devices on curtains, in hemlines, maybe in silk plants. Room service attendants may have been "mic'd up" (microphones on their person or on serving platters). Maintenance people outside the room, doing yard work, cleaning corridors, or shampooing carpeting may be law enforcement personnel blending.

The assignment for Decoy 24 will not be on a grounds crew, housekeeping, or a room service detail. Decoy 24 will be hidden in a sand trap next to a putting green on Hole 4. From that vantage point there are "eyes on" the guest rooms, outside balconies, and patios. Nestled into the sand trap, virtually covered head to toe with sand trap grade sand, the view is clear. From this position everyone can be seen. Wearing desert camouflage, with desert boots on, hair pulled back in a tight ponytail and tucked into a shirt collar, a nylon stocking is pulled over the entire head and face. Vaseline and camo-stick are covering the skull cap and forehead. This will allow for sand to adhere. Goggles for eye protection are worn as well. Hands are disguised with tight-fitting work gloves. As an added technique to insure anonymity, there will be virtually no movement in the sand trap. A water bottle is attached at the waist of the trousers. A flexible plastic drinking tube which runs up from the bottle is taped from the chest up to the chin with non-adhesive surgical tape. The paper tape is comfortable and flexible as well. The water will be refreshing. Decoy 24 is "eyes on."

Within twenty minutes or so of the observation assignment beginning, it appears that a counter surveillance issue has occurred. An individual with binoculars is looking in my direction. He couldn't have made me. Soon the observer calls over a partner, bad guy #2. He glances through the binoculars and shakes his head. He gives back the binoculars to bad guy #1. Bad guy #1 walks off with the binoculars in one hand, down at his side. False alarm. #1 is laughing at something in the room. He raises his right hand, puts his thumb, pointer finger and middle finger together, like a little pyramid, then he shakes his hand over his head. It's a "mama mia" hand gesture. He's handed a bottle of beer, takes a swig, and mingles with other party goers. Decoy 24 is unnoticed.

Cover not blown, the observation detail continues for another hour or so. As dusk appears slowly, you can begin to move extremities. Decoy 24 also knows that when exterior lighting goes on automatically, the observing officer is not silhouetted. What do you know, a couple of rabbits hop in Hole 4 and begin eating their fill of the lush green grass. Rabbit blending.

There were no arrests made and no contact with the group. There were lots of people whose pictures were taken—people in golf outfits, people in silk shirts with tailored trousers and patent leather shoes. There were even occasional un-chaperoned young ladies on hand this weekend. Imagine that!

Summary of Observation Operations: Agencies involved will review all photos and video. Names, aliases, rap sheets, and known associates will all be indexed. Using white boards, chalkboards, computers, photos on bulletin boards and office walls, the investigations team will begin to construct association matrixes. Who knows who, who mingles with whom, and so on. Through the use of visual investigative analysis (via charting), a picture begins to make sense of the relationships. Soon enough, questions like, "Who knows who?" are no longer a mystery. Who said they never flew to the desert from their city of residence or work?

Who says they can't remember being at a country club? Who can't remember dining with a young lady not their wife or girlfriend? The surveillance will prove fruitful in the future. So, here's to you—that is, "lookin' at you, lookin' at me, lookin' at you."

Conclusion:

-Time for a shower

-All optics viewing devices like monoculars, binoculars, and telephoto lenses need to be cleaned, serviced, and recalibrated

-An activity report is completed

-An accounting of all officers involved in the operation is noted. This information is important when preparing a case for trial. You cannot depend on memory to serve you accurately some months or years later.

Decoy 24, "10-7 (out of service) from the detail."

Chapter 10
Deep Cover—Distant Travel

It's a frigid 5:20 a.m. when I walk out of the O'Hare Airport in Chicago, Illinois. This will be an involved and highly dangerous operation for me. By now, I've been in law enforcement for nearly four years. I've received a bachelor's degree and a master's degree over the past five plus years as well. I've employed the discipline I learned from a tour in Vietnam. I've given myself numerous self-criticizing talks to stay grounded. What if there's gunplay? What if you are accused of being a cop? What if your contact doesn't show up? What if your West Coast handler, and the only connection to all that's real and important, loses contact with you? What if you're detained or arrested by an agency that is not "in the loop" and, therefore, you can't divulge who you are?

The aforementioned are just a few of the hundreds of questions I needed answers to for safety and success of an operation, let alone to insure my life wasn't taken by some hoodlum. I thought about exit strategies from rooms and buildings, positions of cover, positions of concealment, and weapon takeaways, the technique used in case someone stuck a gun in my face. (My favorite takeaway tactic, which I practiced over and over, was to see the barrel of a handgun pointed at my head or center torso. I quickly pivot to the left if the shooter is right-handed. I pivot to the right if the shooter is left-handed. On a right-handed shooter, I grab his wrist with my right hand; my left hand grabs the gun's barrel and is pushed outward and turned <u>away from me</u>.

As the weapon is aggressively pushed out, if the shooter has a finger on the trigger, his pointer finger or trigger finger is snapped like a potato chip. The shooter quickly relinquishes the handgun — now it is in my possession.

This idea of a weapon takeaway also poses a new question: am I familiar with the operation of the handgun I wish to take away? Revolver, single shot derringer, or a semi-automatic, they all operate differently. So, I went to a gun dealer and learned how they function. How many rounds in a wheelgun? How many in a .45 caliber? How many in a high capacity 9 millimeter? On and on, the questions don't end. The tactics are practiced over and over. There can be no slight mistakes, no simple errors.

The principals I will associate with over the next couple of days are fond of the Browning Hi Power 9mm. I know the weapon! They're fond of the AK-47. The AK is a Russian-made assault rifle. It's seen action in many theaters from Vietnam to Somalia to Iraq to Afghanistan. Every police officer should be familiar with this long gun. It's a cop killer! Regardless of assignment, police need to learn about this weapon. A few minutes at a gun shop, or with a departmental armorer or weapons instructor is all it takes. Being self-taught, being motivated, and being professional are requirements that hopefully send you home at the end of watch!

So … it's cold. 8° Fahrenheit. I walk across the street and get into a shuttle bus. I'm going to the outskirts of the airport to a cheap hotel. I wish I could stay at the Hilton at the airport, but I settle for a dump called the Red Robin Inn. I check in, pay cash, and go to my room. I unpack my backpack, find my contact's phone number, and then walk to a payphone.

Never be in a position to use a landline that can be traced to you, <u>unless</u> you want to be traced. Today I carry a burner, a throw phone. It's a cheap flip phone that costs $9.99 plus tax. I use phone cards that I buy at drugstores. I favor 120 minute cards priced at $19.99 plus tax. The phone I carry today doubles the phone card minutes. Two hours of phone time becomes four. If I need to throw it away "no big shakes"—it's not an expensive smartphone. For the work I do all I need is a simple flip phone.

I call my contact. He meets me at a café, nothing fancy. We confirm the operation, which will go down tonight on the South Side. I've got an address—it's on at 7:00 p.m. The contact, a detective lieutenant, says, "Nice meeting you, #24. Sort of an odd name."

I say, "If you prefer, lieutenant, you can use my full name."

"Okay, so what's that?" he says.

"Decoy 24, sir."

He replies, "What a ballbuster!"

It's 1900 hours, 7:00 p.m. I'm on a train in downtown Chicago. My stop is at 7:06. I make my way down to the aforementioned address. I'm greeted by a guy called Blade. It's not because he carries one, or is a chef, but rather due to a large cut over his left eyebrow from an injury sustained in Nam.

We exchanged pleasantries; where he was stationed, where I was, so on and so forth. I meet two guys in black berets, both carrying. One has a .38 caliber wheelgun and, whaddayaknow, the other's got a Hi Power 9mm. We discuss my organization membership, MMDM (Movement for a More Democratic Military), STP (Stop The Pig), the SRA (Social Revolution Alliance), and another less well-known organization. We discuss a teach-in strategy at a couple college campuses along with an action plan to provoke police overreaction. Also, the college campuses are a perfect place to eulogize those killed at Kent State University in Ohio and those killed at the hands of the US military machine. This is propaganda at its finest.

We agree to meet again in Cleveland, Ohio in about six weeks. This organization has a national network of very angry people. Even though their anger is justified, the tactics they use don't insulate them from criticism, either. The organization should be familiar to most readers if for no other reason than they were well-covered by national media for years: the Black Panther Party.

Chapter 11
The Heart Must Be Strong, The Skin Must Be Tough, The Mind Must Be Keen

Everyone knows the gun will be loaded. Everyone knows the bomb goes tick-tick. You wanna go undercover? Go on … give it a lick. Just remember, your life will change. You can't go back!

In any career you see so much. You take in an impossible amount of information regardless of the job, whether you're a school teacher, a truck driver, a pediatric radiologist, or an ornamental gardener. The school teacher must be able to distinguish learning strengths and weaknesses displayed by their students. They observe the pupil's eye-hand motor coordination. They test memory skills and retention.

The truck driver learns to anticipate not what the driver just in front of his big rig might do, but the many cars in front of that car. What might they do? They must know how their rig will perform in snow, ice, and extremely hot temperatures. How will the truck perform empty or under a heavy load?

A radiologist who specializes in x-rays of children is called a pediatric radiologist. That doctor must distinguish between what is a normal bone fracture or one possibly caused by an adult that violently twists a child's arm. One is acceptable—the other may reflect those elements of the battered child syndrome. Accident versus child abuse. This doctor must know the limits of a fall so that when someone says, "The baby just fell out of the crib," flags go up. Does the child have the ability to lift itself over a safety rail and, also, could this injury be easily explained by the child's falling say forty two inches onto a carpeted floor? Or is the injury questionable?

Does the gardener trim the plants just before winter or after? Does the gardener trim bushes when he or she wants? Do plants get trimmed on a hot sunny day in July? Do you trim trees with a chain saw, a hack saw, a pruner, or just break the limbs off close to the trunk with bare hands and call it a day?

Lots of questions and considerations for any profession, any job. What are the consequences for a job done incorrectly? A scolding or not getting paid? What if you cause a massive traffic accident? What if the pupil has severe learning problems and cannot be kept in a regular classroom? Try explaining that to the parents and the school principal.

In police work, particularly undercover work, you better be able to "live the lie." You better be able to regain your composure and tuck your PTSD in your pocket for the time being. Your fellow officers expect you to stand tall, "sack up," and hack it! Hardly any, or in my case none of them, will even know you. Some things you witness will remain with you forever. How will you cope? The easy way out is a few beers. Have a couple cocktails. Try the prescription route. Tell your wife or girlfriend, your husband, boyfriend, or a partner you need some alone time. If you didn't come home, were you really alone? Come on now, what were you doing?

Law enforcement agencies do a pitiful job preparing officers for special assignments in general. The selection process is flawed. The training is unsatisfactory or non-existent. Was there a psych review that was done on an UC candidate? Police officers are very apprehensive about anything psych! How often does a department do a "welfare check" on their undercover officers or their SWAT operators? Regular evaluations and, frankly, counseling from an outside professional source are a must!

Anonymity, and nothing less, is required. Much like with any after-action critique or post-shooting critique, the party or parties involved need to be seen. Critical incident stress and special assignment stress are exhausting and can be harmful. The intervention an agency does can save an officer from depression, anxiety, inappropriate professional conduct, drug addition, alcoholism, divorce, and possibly even suicide. Psych reviews should be mandatory.

Behind the vast network of police bureaucracy, there are those forgotten warriors. They don't have the uniform or marked car. They don't have their peers to talk to or those that can offer a recommendation or opinion. Not surprisingly, UC operators are not too chatty about what they do. I told no one. Again, I told no one. When you do go under, you go under, and if you go deep (deep cover) you truly don't identify yourself as a peace officer. So in my case, on numerous occasions, I was detained, arrested, roughed up, and, three times, given a true ass-beating. In all cases, I was confronted by officers when I genuinely looked and acted suspicious. The F.I. (Field Interrogation) quickly turned into a confrontation, being slammed to the ground or into a nearby wall. Not once did I provoke the "tuning up."

On one occasion back east, against my better wishes, I revealed to a deputy chief in a major city that I was "on the job." I was asked to explain my situation. I didn't reveal what agency I worked for, or my real name. Suffice it to say, he got a kick out of "Decoy 24" and he also said his agency would check out the operation I was discussing with him. The following morning I was freed from custody and continued my assignment. (I might share with the reader: I visited this department again about six years later. I had occasion to be a presenter at a few training seminars. At two of those seminars, the same deputy chief introduced me and authenticated my operational background. We had lunch on those two occasions. Small world!)

When a UC is nearly paranoid, it is usually about cover being blown. The other annoyance is hyper-vigilance. You "amp out" and are on a heightened alert to virtually everything. As long as this "being on" doesn't make you sick, it may well heighten tactical awareness. It can also have the opposite effect. If that occurs, then things like interrupted sleep and irritable bowel syndrome pay a visit.

In my training seminars I would break the ice with officers by saying, tongue in cheek, that we will cover numerous topics, some formidable new equipment, and for some of you, "How to quit sleeping with your eyes wide open half the night" or suffering bowel movement episodes that I call "shitting like a goose." Quite often, all kidding aside, there are psychological and physiological considerations to be conscious of in UC work. Returning to the chapter title, UC operators must be strong of heart, have tough skin, and keen minds. We're not talking about forest birds cheeping from an evergreen tree—this is serious.

Chapter 12
A Cast, a VW Bug, and a Dog

Blending sometimes is personal entertainment. The most common question so often asked by customers wishing to "score" (buy) dope or those wishing to sell is, "Are you a cop?" I wished so many times I could belly laugh and fall out of the VW. My response would always be, "Do you think in a 61 VW, with a cast on my left arm, and a Dalmatian dog, I look like a cop?" The response was unanimous, "No, man, but I had to ask." Kinda like Dirty Harry: "I know what you're thinking: 'Did he fire six shots or only five?' Well to tell you the truth in all this excitement I kinda lost track myself. But being this is a .44 Magnum, the most powerful handgun in the world and would blow your head clean off, you've gotta ask yourself one question: 'Do I feel lucky?' Well, do ya, punk?" Only in my case, after they felt sure I was not the man, we did business, they would walk off, and, in short order, be arrested by an apprehension team. They were charged with "holding" (possession), sales, or any number of other offenses.

I bought from other undercover officers—unknown to either party—and sold to UC guys—again unknown to either party. I was detained or arrested by city, county, state, and federal officers; usually released in a couple hours, once Decoy 24 was validated.

On one particular day, I did a buy from a dealer in South Beach: a community of beach goers, surfers, vacationers, homeless people, bikers, skateboarders, other dopers, moms pushing strollers, people walking dogs, and residents. The guy I bought from was arrested within ten minutes. Off he goes to "Happy Jacks Hotel," booking the morning at the county jail annex. The arrest occurred at 10:45 a.m. I'm back at the beach on the pier at 4:30 p.m. buying from the same dude. He had posted bail at 1:30 p.m., took a city bus to the beach, got the rest of his stash from a friend, and "opened the drug store for business" again!

I am back in the same general area again the next day. I break my personal best record: twenty one deals in six hours. The fact that the VW Bug was a very cool car, the dog was legit, and a cast was on my arm, allows for a very productive day. The cast, I might mention, was fitted by Dr. David Greenberg, D.O. Doc Greenberg and I met when we had both stopped to render assistance to the victims of a serious traffic accident. One fatality: a child. I still remember it. Horrific accident. Dr. Greenberg and I became friends that day. We remained friends for over thirty years. He passed away in the fall of 2015. He's affectionately missed.

The days gone by are nothing more than memories. Today's crooks are a potpourri, to be sure. Today's dealers, buyers, and users are so different. The dealers, except small quantity sellers, are armed; the buyers are "moneyed up," except for the poor homeless ones; and many of the personal-use addicts are driving nice vehicles with their dry cleaning hanging neatly on the hanger hooks, groceries in grocery recycle bags, and often an empty car seat in the backseat. Sad, very sad. Those individuals need to be charged with child abuse, neglect, or endangerment in addition to the dope charges.

The risk of dangerous concoctions today is a worry. If it's not the risk of overdose or addiction from OxyContin, "oxy-c," or hydrocodone, "hydro-c," it's the risk from fentanyl and "shard." (*Note*: references define shard and glass as purified methamphetamine, sparkle as mephedrone, and shatter as a marijuana derivative.) There is a difference between medical marijuana and street weed that's designed for extreme highs. That's not to mention the designer drugs that are on the market today, in addition to the pharmaceuticals. We are in a far worse place today in the drug world than at any time in our history. Big statement, but true nonetheless.

The "War on Drugs," "Just Say No," and so many other national programs have had little success, despite politicians touting otherwise and patting themselves on the back. Don't kid yourself—everybody gets a trophy? I don't think so. There are more people dying from drugs today, more drugs coming into the country today, and less measurable resources devoted to drug interdiction today. There is a synthetic drug, a psychoactive derivative called "crumble" in America today. I believe America is on the verge of crumble, itself.

I will tell you that solutions are available, but they may well not be popular. We must have consequences for actions, clearly understood, and clearly implemented. No touchy-feely nonsense, just measurable solutions!

Chapter 13
Psychoactive Resin "Shatters" the Mind

From severe depression to addiction, to poisoning to death, so goes America's attempt at a drug policy. That, of course, is really the indictment of the national policy for crime prevention as well as drug policy for the past fifty years.

Confusion, ineffectiveness, and even hatred are characteristics of far too many who think they have the answers. Really there are just too many bureaucrats, given governmental appointments by governors and the president, and hosts of committees and task forces. Here's a quick glossary of term those in the drug business should know and I would be shocked if those looking to development of state and national drug policy know even three of these terms:

-Pollen
-Shards
-Window panes
-Honey or honeycomb
-Dabbing

-Weed bake
-Shatter
-Rig
-Power pack
-Krokodil (Crocodile)

All of these terms should be common knowledge to "dope cops." They should be known to DARE officers working on high school campuses. Those on patrol in crime-ridden neighborhoods where drugs are prevalent should know these terms. How can a simple substance like pot be hyper-concentrated? How do water pipes vaporize their substances? Can you do anything to a marijuana bud to get a better high? Can you have a high-less experience with marijuana?

I have consulted for hundreds of law enforcement agencies across the country and provinces in Canada, visited Costa Rica to do training, and been to the most prestigious law enforcement training facilities in the USA. We are "slippin" in our war on crime. We aren't even familiar with street hoodlums' language. An example: a group of gang members in a nice ride (nice car), an Escalade or larger series BMW, drive into a wealthy community. With the windows tinted and four or five of the hoodlums in the vehicle crouched down, the driver obeys all traffic laws. They cruise in a careful manner then pull into a drive way of a target home. It will be ransacked in a matter of minutes then off goes the vehicle, slow and safe, so not to raise suspicion. The car looks like it belongs in the neighborhood. The driver waits with the vehicle. His five passengers exit and aggressively hit the house: stereos, jewelry, big screen TVs, art pieces—gone in a flash. Many times thieves actually discard their sweatshirts (hoodies) and put on ball caps or take off their ball caps, so the home security systems capture a picture of people running around in certain apparel that's no longer worn during the careful and law-abiding getaway. This technique used to be called "smotherin,'" now "mobbing." Tossing clothes off is "changing your uniform."

You must know the enemy or criminal to deal with them effectively. Leave the badge-heavy anger and hatred on the shelf. Conduct that's unbecoming by officers can quickly atrophy, if not rot, the human conscience. Officers must be highly trained. It's mandatory as far as I'm concerned.

Hard core bad guys do exist! They make me sick. They cook up lethal concoctions that kill people. These individuals only care about money. Imagine logging into evidence over eight thousand dollars in pocket cash from a teenager. I don't imagine it, I've seen it.

Uneducated kids from across the border in Mexico often have no future. Many turn to crime. Most of the youthful populations in the countries we call "terrorist prone" are unemployed. The point: There is no future for so many young people. There's really no temptation regarding the drift toward criminality for these kids. There simply is no alternative. They would rather transport drugs, do assassinations, and do butane and propane extractions of weed than live in a village where there's no future.

I remember a saying that if you give a man a fish, you feed him for a day; teach a man to fish and you feed him for a lifetime. Today's thugs rob the fish store, beat the counter service employees, empty the cash register, grab some chips and soda, and enjoy every minute of it.

Chapter 14
Decoy 24 Does Raid Planning

Remember the acronym, RAID (Reconnaissance, Assault plan, Intelligence, Deploy the squad). Most extensive investigations revolving around narcotics, gangs, and even terrorism will at some point require the development of a raid plan.

Having done the front end work, that is, following criminals, identifying the customers, associates, and often family members, the plan is important and must be thoroughly thought through. I was in the Midwest some years ago evaluating a raid gone wrong. The department had great, but inexperienced, personnel. They were motivated but did not possess the knowledge to take into consideration anything that might go wrong. Things do go wrong.

The location to be hit was on the outskirts of town. There was always train traffic in the early morning and early afternoon hours. If the road that led to the nearest, and only, hospital was blocked by a signal crossing, medical attention would be significantly delayed. Sure enough, an officer slipped and fell in his haste to get into position. His ankle was broken. Not a crisis but, nonetheless, the medical attention was delayed. Next, an officer was shot and wounded on approach to the house. The acronym APES should be understood: **A**pproach to the **P**osition of entry to prepare to **E**nter and **S**earch. The officer's injury was not life-threatening. However, two officers needed medical assistance. The fire department was on one side of the signal, the injured officers on the other side. The train was rambling along at 15 mph or so … and the train had 86 cars. Do the math! Eventually the exchange was made of the shooting victim to paramedics with the fire department. The officer with the ankle injury was chauffeured by a marked car.

The plan should have placed the fire department's EMTs or paramedics two blocks or so from the battle problem. The train traffic issue should have been addressed when the raid plan was being developed. Same goes with felony warrant service. The more dangerous the arrest issues, the more complex — not confusing, but complex — and thorough the arrest plan.

I could go on and on. Officers going to the wrong house, arresting the wrong people, shooting the wrong dog (one that posed no threat for example), not having enough personnel … In Northern California, a farmhouse was going to be assaulted. No one bothered to check on large chains that were used to secure a heavy metal gate. No one noticed the cameras attached to a pole below a weather vane. The fence was electrified on the entire front. Solution: don't approach the front. There was an irrigation ditch on the west side. Careful now, the ditch and irrigation stream had a couple feet of water in it. The back of the farmhouse was unsatisfactory due to the large number of flood lights that lit up the backyard and an outbuilding. The east side of the farm house was bordered by a dear old couple. They had little patience with their gangland neighbors. That's the safe side, plus you have a team potentially out of the elements who can have "eyes on" the suspect location before and during the raid.

I might as well give you one more example of poor planning: The target consisted of right-wing extremists in their compound. It was heavily fortified. There were six sentries on the outer perimeter, two more on the front porch, three in a Toyota Land Cruiser, and two manning a front gate that was lit up like an airfield. That's fourteen people outside of the compound. The approach team was eight officers. Only half of the officers were equipped with long guns. Inside the compound's meeting house were approximately twenty more people. There were signs all over posting "No Trespassing," "No Entry," and "We Kill Cops." No operation was conducted that evening. Surveillance is great, but assault operations: "Negatory" (no).

Tactical regrouping is not defeat. It's the smarter option. The bad guys will be bad tomorrow, and the next day, and the next. Officers are one bad decision away from "all hell broke loose," "I don't know happened," and so on.

Sometimes in our modern world, I think instinct has been lost or it's sorely lacking. Faulty problem assessment, inadequate training, or inappropriate gear are all excuses for tactical failure. The underlying factors of failed operation in a "lessons learned" critique are almost always the same: There was a deviation from proper policy guidelines, or no policy guidelines existed. There was a lack of effective leadership. There has been no mentoring of less experienced officers. Nothing takes the place of the single-eye that safeguards us from conflict, confusion, and chaos.

During my writing of this book, there have been numerous executive personnel, like chiefs of police, fired because their personnel made tragic mistakes. Again, the department's policies were not followed or policies were lacking. There is no excuse for error. Executive development training seldom addresses policy revision or police guidelines that focus on tactical situations. That needs to change.

Chapter 15
On Vacation ... Really!

There are far too many officers who are pressed into service while on vacation, enjoying a day off, at their child's soccer game, or even on a date.

This is a circumstance that occurred to me while I was vacationing with my wife. I share it with you, chucking, probably because my wife's not peering over my shoulder as I'm writing.

Her ancestors were family farmers outside of Rome, not far from the Tuscany region. If you have a chance to visit Italy sometime, make a point to get out of the city of Rome for some fresh air, beauty, and friendly faces offering you pizza that's out of this world, eggplant parmesan, delicate dessert items, and wines that are delicious.

Prior to going into Rome, my wife and I decide to visit Venice for three days. We fly to Venice, get a hotel, visit glass-blowing shops, observe wood craftsmen constructing gondolas, and admire St. Mark's Basilica—a Catholic church of extraordinary beauty. We visit a great little café on the canal called *Osteria ai 40 Ladroni* or "The Restaurant of the 40

Thieves." It is a nod to the many pirates long ago. Everything from great salads and fresh fish entrees to incredible pastas can be found here.

On day four, we check out of the hotel and take a shuttle to the train station. We acquire our one-way tickets to Rome, about a three hour trip. I purchased first class seating. Frankly the cost was only $30 more per person for a larger reclining seat in a far less congested car.

As we hustle down to Platform #5, I am impressed to see a sleek, modern train. The colors are brilliant and bright: red with silver and white highlights. When we walk down the cement corridor to Car 6, I notice three uniformed police officers of the Venice Municipal Police. I stop to say hello and my wife goes up to the car stairway to board. One of the officers speaks English fairly well and explains, "American cop" to them. We all smile and I tell them, "Be safe and be tactical." They give me bigger smiles and tell me, "Ciao, American cop!" I board, find my wife, and tell her I'm going to bring our three suitcases in off of the corridor.

I hoist one up to the train car floor, go down and get the second, then go and bring the third on board. I am greeted by a guy, about 30 years old, 160-170 pounds, dark haired, and wearing dark shorts with a short sleeve shirt. He's stowed the first suitcase and has the second one in his hand. I thank him for his help and I push the third one under my compartment seat. He now approaches me and says, "20

Euro to help you." That's about $20 American for three or four minutes of shoving a few suitcases around.

I stand up and say to him, "What did you just say?" He says, "20 Euro. I helped you." I have a quick mental flash: no train personnel I saw had shorts or a sports shirt on. I've been had! I ask him, "Who do you work for: Trenitalia or some gang?" He sees that I'm hot! He backs up slowly, then turns around and moves toward Car 5. I watch the automatic doors open and close as he leaves our car and goes into the next. As he slips into Car 5 he quickly grabs a passenger's overhead luggage. He continues looking back at me, grabs a lady's shoulder purse (can you believe it?), and then sees me in foot pursuit.

He runs through Car 4 into Car 3. I'm on his behind, afterburners on. He's mine! He runs out of Car 3, throws the luggage down, and starts running toward the train station. (I shouldn't boast, but I have a high school letter in track as well as one in basketball.) I'm running and he's sunk.

I hear men yelling, "American cop! Look, American cop!" My peripheral vision picks up three Venezia uniforms, short legs chuggin' on the next platform over. I've got his collar, he's going down. There's nothing more I can do — I certainly don't have jurisdiction. Another ten or twelve train employees are now gathered around me. Soon three uniformed officers are on the scene. There's lots of hectic craziness going on with intermittent "American cop" verbiage. He's cuffed by Italian authorities. We all again smile. I whisper into the suspect's ear the importance of good behavior and I now turn to go back to Car 6. My Italian friends and the train personnel wave vigorously. I hear, in Italian, then English, "All aboard Trenitalia #173 to Rome. All aboard!"

I join my wife, who glares at me and says "On vacation, really?! Can you please give it a rest?"

Outcome: Got the stink eye for a few more minutes as we left the station. Then the couple who were reunited with their luggage came into Car 6. Right, to thank me! Also, a number of train personnel came by my seat and smiled. American cop. Good job! I glanced at my wife a couple times saying, "American cop. I'm looking out for your people." She shook her head and hid her face behind her magazine. She loved it.

Saint Michael Police Prayer

Saint Michael, heaven's glorious commissioner of police, who once so neatly and successfully cleared God's premises of all its undesirables, look with kindly and professional eyes on your earthly force.

Give us cool heads, stout hearts, and uncanny flair for investigation and wise judgment.

Make us the terror of burglars, the friend of law-abiding citizens, strict with law-breakers and impervious to temptations.

You know, Saint Michael, from your own experiences with the devil that the police officer's lot on earth is not always a happy one; but your sense of duty that so pleased God, your hard knocks that so surprised the devil, and your angelic self-control give us inspiration.

And when we lay down our night sticks, enroll us in your heavenly force, where we will be as proud to guard the throne of God as we have been to guard the city of all people.

Amen.

(Verified by the United States Catholic Church, this prayer was approved by Pope Leo XIII in 1884.)

Acknowledgements

James would like to thank:

- Theresa Andreen for her hard work in the first editing.

- Justin Aubrey for his exceptional artwork and graphics.

- Randy Beck with My Domain Tools for his help with website development.

- A. Wm. Davis for his I.T. assistance.

- D. Davis for her assistance with research.

He particularly wishes to thank Mr. Glen Aubrey with Creative Team Publishing for his diligent efforts following up on details to make this project happen.

About the Author

A little boy grows up in a Midwestern farm town. He spends many of his childhood days pushing a red wagon up a small hill, then jumping in it and steering it furiously down that hill. All the time he dreams of being a police officer. Remember, "Don't quit your day dream." By high school, he's transplanted to the West Coast. His senior year of high school he attends a Career Day. He decides once again to become a police officer. He studies police science at college and hopes to continue his education towards his bachelor's degree … but Vietnam comes calling!

He is dramatically affected by President Kennedy's statement in a speech to the nation: "ask not what your country can do for you—ask what you can do for your country." He enlists, volunteers for Vietnam, does a tour in Vietnam, and eventually he's back in the USA and back in college.

He'll finish a bachelor's degree, a master's, and work on a doctorate. He'll work at the county and state levels in the law enforcement profession. From working cases he'll eventually move into advanced field training. He'll be acknowledged in the journal, *Outstanding Young Men of America*, (1977).

He'll lecture at three different universities. Over a period of time, he will receive numerous commendations, including the Medal of Merit for Heroism.

He continues to speak publically throughout the country. He enjoys spending time with his family, is active in his community, and does volunteer work for his church and for disabled veterans.

About the Book

Decoy 24 is a collection of short stories. These stories examine the multiple aspects of criminality in society. The reader will explore the criminal values revealed by those who hate society, those willing to risk it all for pitiful gains while many times sacrificing their own lives.

These vignettes paint a picture of street violence and look at the underbelly of the narco-pariah that is multiplying every day.

Decoy 24 also was the call sign used by the author during his many undercover operations. His name was not spoken, to guarantee some measure of anonymity. In the book, Decoy 24 is referenced frequently, both when he is broadcasting over a frequency of the radio and when he might need to reveal who he was when working with law enforcement agencies that did not know him. His comrades in law enforcement and the general public are both informed of the insidious problem of criminal behavior in our society.

Whether it's a street, prison or outlaw motorcycle gang, organized crime syndicate, or as a lone wolf, Decoy 24 has had first-hand experience in infiltrating a number of criminal organizations which provided him and the reader with knowledge that only a few people could obtain.

This book acknowledges the sacrifices made by many men and women unknown and working now as undercover operators. City, county, state, and federal agencies all play their part in confronting the menace of such horrific social violence.

At this writing, the author wishes to acknowledge all those officers that are on the rolls of LEOKA. The acronym stands for "Law Enforcement Officers Killed and Assaulted."

Albert Einstein said: "Only a life lived in the service to others is a life well lived." Certainly our LEOKA community has lived that life.

Services

Fee-based guest speaking engagements and tuition-based seminars are available upon request.

Please visit www.Decoy24.com for additional information.

Book Order Form

Please send me #_____ copies of *Decoy 24*
                    A Glimpse at the Undercover Operations of Law Enforcement

Quantity #_____ x $19.95 each (applicable taxes, shipping, & handling *included*)
= Total $_____

Method of Payment:

☐ Check enclosed payable to James R. Davis.

☐ Charge my account (Visa or Mastercard only)
      Credit Card Account Number:

☐☐☐☐ – ☐☐☐☐ – ☐☐☐☐ – ☐☐☐☐

      Expiration Date: ☐☐ – ☐☐
      Signature of Card Holder_____
      Date_____

Shipping Name_____

Address_____

City, State, Zip_____

Phone number should we wish to contact you: (_____)_____

Please mail completed order form and checks or credit card information to:

James R. Davis
2840 Fletcher Parkway, #207
El Cajon, CA 92020
United States

You may also order online at www.Decoy24.com.

CPSIA information can be obtained
at www.ICGtesting.com
Printed in the USA
FFOW03n1203290817
39395FF